snipped tales

#snippedtales

Published in paperback in 2016 by Sixth Element Publishing
on behalf of Julie Kirk

Sixth Element Publishing
Arthur Robinson House
13-14 The Green
Billingham TS23 1EU
Tel: 01642 360253
www.6epublishing.net

© Julie Kirk 2016

ISBN 978-1-908299-74-1

British Library Cataloguing in Publication Data. A catalogue record for this book is
available from the British Library.

Printed in Great Britain.

withjuliekirk.com

snipped tales

julie kirk

With illustrations by Kirsty Neale

To James.

Because whenever I, or my scissors, break,
you always do your best to mend us.

contents

chapter 4 - brief encounters

chapter 5 - oh my!

chapter 6 - minor mythologies

chapter 7 - refreshments will be served

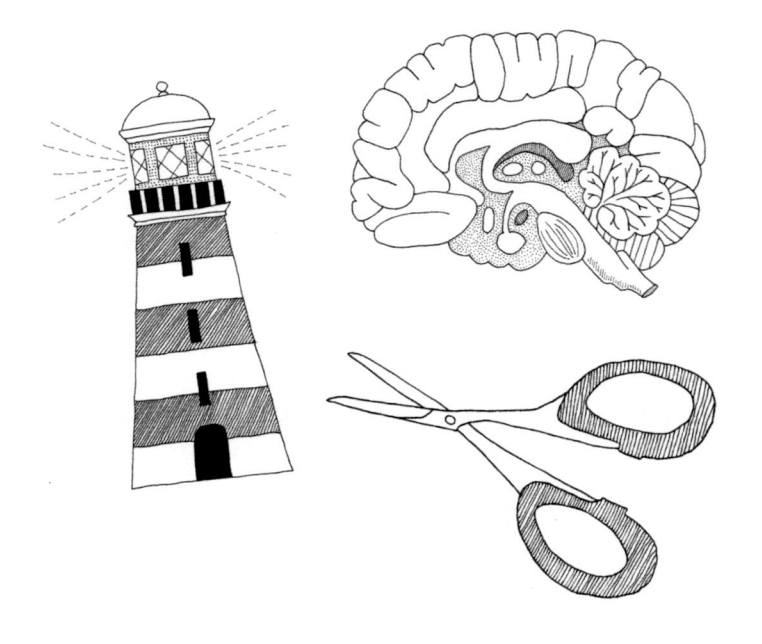

chapter 1
being human

Lost Property Office.

Here we look after
some of the things
other people have lost.

Things like —

pencils

jewellery

a series of debates

a sense of chivalric romance,

a waist ; a mind;

nerves

cherries,

each other

everything

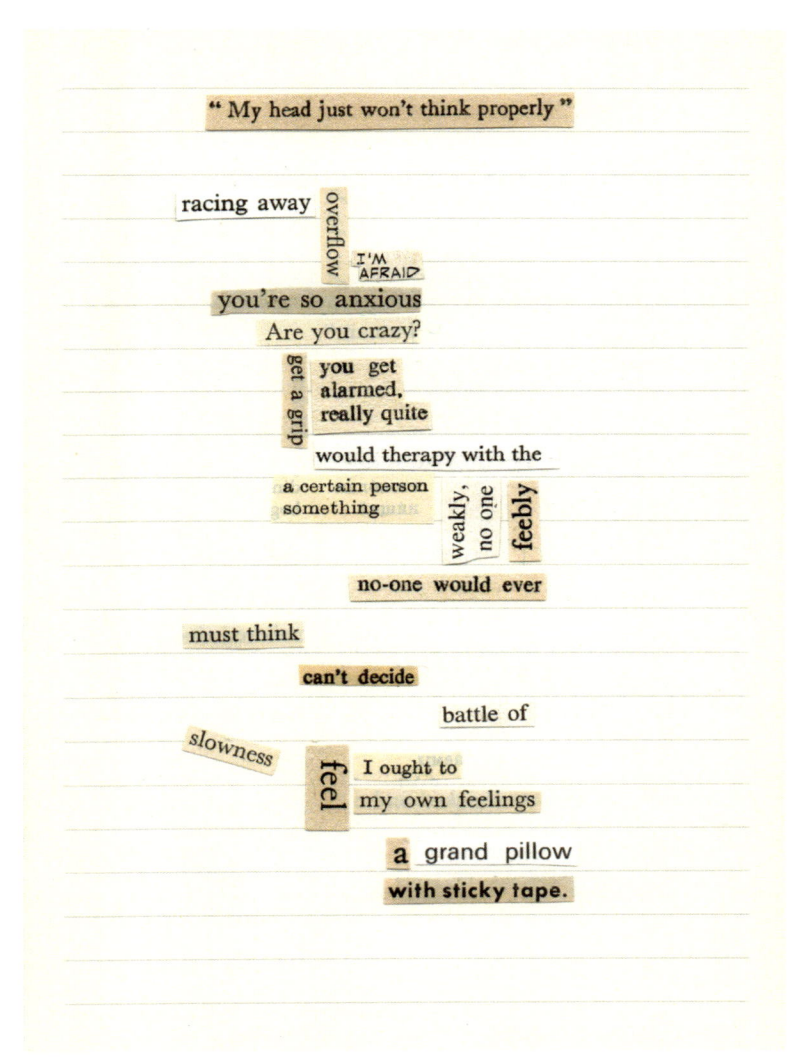

" My head just won't think properly "

racing away overflow

I'M AFRAID

you're so anxious

Are you crazy?

get a grip you get alarmed, really quite

would therapy with the

a certain person something

weakly, no one feebly

no-one would ever

must think

can't decide

battle of

slowness

feel I ought to my own feelings

a grand pillow

with sticky tape.

DROWNING.

Water above and water around

it would be easy to slip down
                        breathless,

into

the wide-ness of the sea;

Lighthouse

When a man is teetering

on the brink of **leaving the land-** scape

face in **the wind**

brain in free fall,

a tentative foot over the edge

           struggling

Between

the violet-green seas,

and a

blackness, so wide and deep

Then

For love of life, in fear and trembling,

switch on **your** lamp

while you can,

and at least give him a chance

to save himself

Duties of Relatives.

to visit those who are ill and infirm.

to listen

To accept

to Take hold of your hand

to cushion the heart,

and

to engage in

worrying,

Treatment.

Put on your things and go out for a walk

Go to the seaside,

have a small soft cake

breathe

dream

dance again.

You might as well

PREPARING FOR DORMANCY

Choose an out-of-the-way place

Turn off all appliances

say your car has broken down

draw the bed-curtains and

cultivate the dim and silent.

Then

saunter

slowly

into the hands of the Sandman

Plans for Sunday *Afternoon*

museum
music
wash
think

Each one of us is inside a big paper bag.

and **the** type of person you are going to be throughout life
is in large measure dependent on what you do
about that

Some move all over the world taking the bag with
them every single day!
some are able to make extra space inside for a stool,
where they can sit and read.
and others, cut the bag with scissors or shears
to escape the whole business,

And then there are those who
go splashing in puddles   til the paper
is sodden and then they only have to lift it slightly
with trembling fingers, to get free.

when a player plays out all his cards

a space is left,

one of hesitation, dissatisfaction , doubt

However,

Just as a swimmer needs to get into the water, so
the player may take a new pack and

draw the top card.

A Trip

I am going to take a walk.

I am going to keep on the road

    I may lose my way
And myself.

But hey

The distances are not too great,

and after all,

even the wrong road always leads somewhere.

" self-balancing "

have two buttocks on a chair.

Practise holding **on** to some tea, or a drink in one hand and a **good** book in the other,

"Well done!"

Now repeat as often as possible.

chapter 2
a life documented

'The Unknown Bird'

You need to find out what
your character's like.
Then learn to accept yourself
and things as they are.

you don't have to be
everything to everyone.

No one ever saw an owl picking cherries

And owls are Okay with that

sense of balance.

The missing man
sat on one end of the seesaw and
looked hard at the little girl.

She stared back.
and put three stones from the play-pit
and an apple on the other end.

They balanced

Margot

The next time you see her
waiting at the bus stop
finger-tips bent over her walking stick
or sitting up in bed, propped with pillows,
or tentatively dusting china ornaments
it is important to remember
that back

in

her

day

she was called the *Butterfly*
a fully-qualified pilot,
who the soldiers in the bar voted

'most likely to cause trouble indoors.'

'Local Boy Makes Good'

It was a warm evening on the beach
the sea was far out,
and a thin young man
lay on his back
surrounded by high palm trees.

Shading his eyes from the glare of the sun,
he got up to pour more brandy and
sniffed the sea air having forgotten all about
the old plaster
dust sheets
pieces of board and scraps of tin,
he had left many a mile behind in another world.

Another life

Another man

He did not

She didn't.

But we did.

And they did.

The Employee

As the only employee left at
International Telephone & Telegraph

Bobby saw his chance
to
Finally
at long last
take his place as
business executive
of the month

Genetics.

with folding ribs and

arms which can be unscrewed once he is older

he was a source
of constant worry to his mother,

top notes

as he opened the french windows
Alf couldn't quite make up his mind
if the smell in the kitchen was left over
from the fumigation – or if Prunella
had been trying out another of her
exclusive perfumes.

20

Trinity

Anne went very red
when she **noticed** that
in the woolly **bodice** she had
knit for Fulbert

the arm-holes *outnumbered*
the neck-holes
3 to 1.

A gathering of people

A trip when walking

A small bushy area

awkward.

chapter 3
i'm just saying

I know what you're thinking,
(mainly because **unasked** you tell me)

You think **I'm** very uncertain and slight,
that **I dance about** flapping
because I'm a bit scared about all this.
and that I should
stop being a whimsical bloody fool and
force myself to change
Well, thank you very much but you're wrong.

There is **no** remedy for my character
no cure for my habit of growth
no therapy **for my** daily weather
and
my
heart's core doesn't need your approval.

AIRWAYS

A snake

knives

untruths

These are dangerous if they
are swallowed

a suitable vacancy

Knowing the truth at last,
He left five minutes ago.

waving goodbye.

Critique:

Write it once more.
Write it once more, please,

say the same thing in different words

A HOLIDAY ABROAD

My glasses are broken.

The heating is on and

I have not bought any-
thing during my stay.

I have blisters, a sore throat

and I am overtired.

I am suffering from sunburn.

I have been bitten by an insect.

And I think I have food poisoning.

wish you were here

sightseeing on
wild-west ponies.

listen

I'm not really interested
in shopping for Souvenir-gifts.

just

take me to the places
where cowboys celebrated

NEW LOOK

Sarah looked at him with contempt and left the room.

In the sitting-room she mixed herself a whisky and soda.

She didn't want a party.
She didn't want bows

She wanted claws.

past Regrets and future Fears

For a wild minute he had wanted
to change his way of living entirely,
and surge forward to a better life!

But everything seemed the same.

Everything.

Life's unending treadmill

During the last few years of my
spirited, rebellious youth,

I thought that
I'd never stop kicking
But now . . .

my legs are not so young
as they used to be!

An insult
in compact form

your mother

chapter 4
brief encounters

separated bodies

Where **we** are :

One space before and one space after.

Where I want us to be :

No space before and no space after.

The pledge

right where you are,

I'll be

Escape Velocity

Let's go away.

Let's go (there).

the hold

before now she had only ever been
held by competent men at best.

But when he took her in his arms the feeling
was something like a bird flying,

at 100 miles per hour
and running right into .the inner edge of
hurricane;

She could feel the gravitational field folding in
softly around them.

And for months afterwards
she went on feeling as graceful as forked lightning
as powerful as Artemis, goddess of the hunt.

And as beautiful as the lotus flower.

"How long will this job last, a long time?"

"What time's your train?

perhaps **you'd** like to spend another night?"

Guy made no comment.

"**I know** I shan't be able to see you
as much as I'd like. But we'll keep *in touch* by
writing. I'll write you notes **and** letters and
I shall send parcels "
(I choked over the last words.)
And **Guy tried to speak but** I
swiftly handed **him** all the things I thought
would **keep him close,**
A pen ... some writing paper, some envelopes
... some postcards, some stamps. My heart ...
And in return ? He gave me back my pen.

He who hesitates

She turned and faced him,
here, in the corridor
jammed together

They smiled

He asked her about herself

She felt exposed

He stood quite still,
for fear of being swept overboard
and decided not to make the first move.

Neither of them enjoyed the party.

Whom did he marry?

His scruples being thus overcome by the concussion

Captain Mason

leant forward

and **said**

" I'm afraid I've *forgotten* your name

but . . .

My wife says, that I love you more than

anything else in the world,

and you know it."

Arabella Jane smiled at him, a little mockingly,

"Of course I know," She laughed.

"Well . . ." said the Captain

his mouth was smiling and his eyes held hers.

" may I take *you* home, instead? "

Middle Ages

About a month after the two had met,

Benedick's infatuation for the flame of his heart
was dying out . In the beginning
incredulous of his luck, (and moved by lust,)
he had remained composed
when she **giggled** at his poetry .

Then , **with** great effort said nothing
when **she** declared She was allergic to Shakespeare

But he was finally forced to put a stop to
the fantasy when she referred to
the 1990s as
. . .

'the olden days'

'a born bachelor.'

Fred has just shown Joan a dead rat.

in view of this she did *not* feel

he was quite what Mother

would call

husband material

chapter 5
oh my!

DILEMMAS

The force of attraction between bodies

the distance between the parallel planes

Wanting what belongs
to another

the triangles

No regrets

It's wrong, and

I *know* it's wrong.

And yet

43

BED-MAKING

To warm a bed

place the electric blanket under the bottom sheet

Before bumping into each other like fury!

TIES THAT BIND

Minty, who had freed herself from the skip-
ping-rope with ease,

smiled as she was

bound with insulating tape to the

four-poster bed with curtains round it

When Giles

came towards her, kissing her forehead lightly

she asked

nonchalantly,

"You don't mean at your age you don't even know
what handcuffs are?"

" Or why not use the cellar as a cellar
and take up making home-made wine as a hobby? "

something told Mr Turner
that Mrs Turner
wasn't quite as excited about
his plan for a naughty dungeon
as he was.

A mis understanding at Halstead Manor.

Lily gasped.
"No, Grandmama she interrupted

" Lady Saintbury said she fell for Sir Wimbold because he was a rather fine pianist!"

MORE WAYS TO MEASURE

Leading an abstracted, scholarly life,
he was ill-fitted for common worldly affairs.

and yet

by means of being in possession of

a kind heart
a handsome **library**
and a very big pocket in his trousers,

Miss Spencer's nephew
was never ever short of **eager**
young lady **companions**

IN 3 WORDS.

broad   sonorous
deep   keen-sighted
dear   handsome

big-eyed   pitiful
huge   hot
ill-natured   thin

filthy   stiff
smooth   quiet
loud   firm

reddish   cry-baby, sniveller
slightly bitter drunkard
bluish

Casanova there

told himself that he had better make

more of an effort with

his on line dating profile

49

straight-from-the-shoulder advice

If the knees are crossed
dating is more difficult.

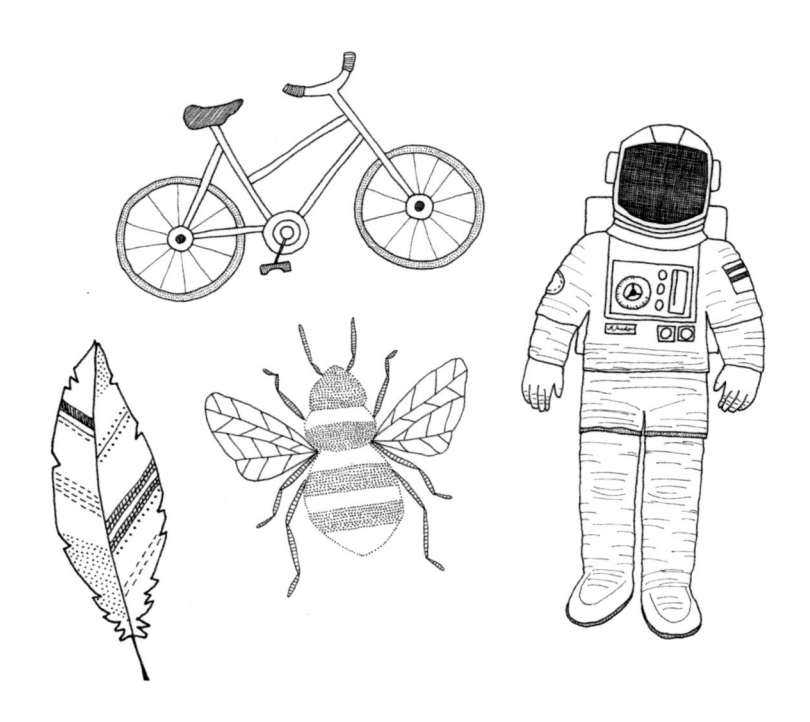

chapter 6
minor mythologies

LEGEND

Adults over-winter in crevices and

those who have cars get into their cars and stay in them[1].

They grow because they *eat* food.

These are the people who

are submerged in the accessories of style and fashion

They make

dance floors for themselves in the forest.

Where

between them they

do a great deal of dancing and strutting

All in all,

Grown-ups do exactly as they like

THE HISTORY OF LIFE ON EARTH

Into this Universe,

       children ride bicycles

            willy-nilly

    without fear

And as with frightened horses and rain showers

We can't

   turn

    nor steer them the way we want

Gravity

What if

as a result of a careless shot

or an unlucky bounce

the first astronauts

hit the ceiling. . .?

Stuffed eggs

Anyone falling from a height towards the

ground

feels the

Oh!

Oh-h-h-h-h-h!!!

heels

over head sensation

familiar to

Humpty Dumpty

The Great Egg Carton Crusades

It had **been** the rainiest of evenings
the time the Knights of the Cardboard Castle
fought the egg box dragon

It blew hard all that night,
and in the morning
all that remained on the battle field
was a thick
layer of **paper** mache

THE LAST
Gentleman Standing

Although there were many men eager

to overcome the monster

it could never be him. when he got there

he could almost reach out and touch it

but he didn't . It looked tired

tormented , wounded

a mere fragment ;

a damaged and groaning figure

whose fighting spirit had been torn apart,

Without a second thought.

the gentle, virtuous Smith changed his mind

turned round

and instead

found triumph

in

walking

away

Free Fall

He was still eligible, a wealthy unmarried man in his early fifties.

In newspapers and on radio and television,
perhaps the best liked man ever

and a semi-monumental type

Gradually he *learned how to cope*

with projecting wings

the sensation of being weightless,

the circling high over

the earth

and the bright-coloured feathers.

Ornament

The more ambitious male birds of paradise

asked for a woolly scarf

· if permitted by fashion,

to be really distinct from any other birds

the life of a frog

There's the

long immersion in a pond or stream and the

small funny, green *bulging* body,

then, of course,

When the feet are placed together

the space separating the ankles is abnormally wide,

but

at least you get

to kiss **your** fair *share*

of princesses

THE GREAT ALLIANCE

Apart from the occasional elephant and top hat
half hidden in the long grass,
all the horses, cages, tigers and caravans
were packing up to join another circus
when Aunt Barbara recognised that she was
unable to resist life in the big top. And soon
New troops of rats, mice, guinea pigs, cats and dogs
clawless lobsters, tinted jellyfish, luminous lantern-
fishes with shining light pores, small herring-like fishes,
purple swimming crabs, three monkeys
a whole troop of wild asses, another monkey
and several other things too were lined up

They even added a bee a giraffe
and Lulu the spaniel
(the world famous fire juggler)
So the show went on.

'Set me any task, I'll gladly prove myself,'

said the Greek hero,

taking up his sword and crossbow,

full of lofty intention

'Very well, you shall have your chance.'

declared EURYSTHEUS

"How about you *take* a hard, bitter journey

to the Tundra Lands of the Old World

spend the night at the house of the ogre and then ...

stick out your neck and wings angrily; cluck and
puff your feathers out; or stagger away?"

It was at this stage in the trial that HERCULES

began to *suspect*

that the King was *running* out of *ideas*

chapter 7
refreshments will be served

The Weekend begins

Seven o'clock.

Wine, glass of.   Please

At a quarter to nine.

El vino,   Thank you.

At half past nine

Red wine, white wine.

El vino tinto, blanco.

Actually   **Just** give me any

old thing as long as it's vino.

11 o'clock   Wine, a bottle of wine.

gracias.

RECREATIONS

At breakfast the next morning
All the sailors had
indigestion and headaches,
bruises and gout.

and

a charge of bad manners

fungi intolerance

Roger saw some mushrooms on the side of the road.
"I'm crazy about' mushrooms. Let's pick some.
and we'll eat them this evening."

"Pick all the mushrooms you wish", answered John,
"and eat them. *I* shall not eat any."

"Why?" asked Roger.

" Because I once knew a professor of botany⁵ who
had spent his life⁶ studying mushrooms.
And Do you know how the poor man died?

"mushroom poisoning⁷..." Roger suggested.

"No, he . . . er . . . he passed a toad stool"

A phone call from *camp*

"Yes, Esther. Thank you,

We've got more **than** enough

beans, enough to supply the whole
world for three years in *fact*.

"Very well," she replied,

" I'll just

Bring some more toast. "

Shakespeare's writing.
Jane Austen, sandwiches and cream tea
with a few flowers in jam-jars,
fine cups, saucers and plates
The boat race or *Cricket* and the 1966 World Cup,
A little time to spare for a genial discussion
the weather (that black cloud !)
and where the dreadful noise is coming from !

A blackbird,
cooking smells
minstrels and jesters
poetry, hamsters and Victorian things.
history.
security.

Freedom

and the use of an umbrella

Today's Special

eating in Britain is particularly complex,

Sometimes

We're having fruit salad, and cream, sardines, plum cake, éclairs and chocolate mousse.

or it might be many kinds of roast meat

or Pieces of pie (lemon meringue, apple,

shepherd's)

or a tea-party with the usual smattering

of sandwiches egg-custard and preserves, etc.

However, at other times we're dining on

titbits

such as sea bass served with a cloud of Brazilian coffee

pieces of meat stewed in melting snow

and rich organic elk poached in a light tetanus serum

on rye bread

Hidden features.

Sally secretly loves biscuits

She glues them to the underside
of her body and carries them around with her

at work to prevent the possibility

of *having* to eat

yoghurt or fruit

at dinner-time.

DIGESTION

After exchanging
an apple
for a dictionary

Little Polly
must have eaten all
the definitions

SPECIAL THANKS

To all the dusty shelves and jumbled rummage boxes of books whose pages I've recast into my stories, treasure-seeking for new narratives in amongst the old has been a delight.

To Kirsty Neale for not only illustrating my tales with love and care but for her understanding, advice, and friendship. And to Gillie and Graeme at Sixth Element Publishing for their work on getting this book out of my hands and into yours.

To my craft and cake-loving friends for their crafts, cakes, and companionship... and for always telling me I should write a book.

To the lovely people who've visited and supported my blog over the years for introducing me to the gift of having my words find an audience... and for always telling me I should write a book.

And to my much loved family for not only always telling me I should write a book... but for loyally and unfalteringly believing that I actually could.

You see? I do listen to what you all tell me to do. Sometimes.